This book belongs to
_____

Martin Luther King, Jr.

By Mary Nhin

Illustrated By
Yuliia Zolotova

This book is dedicated to my children - Mikey, Kobe, and Jojo.

Copyright © 2021 by Grow Grit Press LLC. All rights reserved. No part of this book may be reproduced in any form without permission in writing from the publisher. Please send bulk order requests to growgritpress@gmail.com 978-1-63731-317-6 Printed and bound in the USA. MiniMovers.tv

Hi, I'm Martin Luther King, Jr.

When I was younger, I played outside with the children in my neighborhood. Luckily for me, my best friend was just across the street from me.

When we both turned six, we were sent to separate schools. This is because he was white, and I was black.

This was a time when segregation existed in America, a practice requiring separate housing, education and other services for people of color.

That hurt me a lot.

I missed my friend. I began to get very upset at the world. During this time, my parents taught me the importance of forgiveness and the Christian belief in loving all people.

Despite all of the things happening, my parents firmly believed in equality, and encouraged me to challenge the racism wherever I could.

We must accept finite disappointment,
but never lose infinite hope.

When I grew older, I went to college to study to join the ministry. It was here that I met a woman I grew to love, but I was forced to call off the relationship because we were different races.

I was warned that I could never be a pastor if I had an interracial marriage.

After this, I promised to myself that I would do everything I could to end racism in America.

After an African American woman named Rosa Parks was arrested for refusing to give up her seat on the bus for a white man, I agreed to lead the Montgomery Bus Boycott.

In this protest, we came together and refused to take the bus until the bus company ended their racism.

I gave a speech called *I Have a Dream* that many people resonated with.

All of these events eventually led to the passing of the Civil Rights Act of 1964, which ended racial segregation in America.

I have a dream that my four little children will one day live in a nation where they will not be judged by the color of their skin but by the content of their character.

I say to you today, my friends, so even though we face the difficulties of today and tomorrow, I still have a dream. It is a dream deeply rooted in the American dream.

I have a dream that one day this nation will rise up and live out the true meaning of its creed: "We hold these truths to be self-evident: that all men are created equal."

I have a dream that one day on the red hills of Georgia the sons of former slaves and the sons of former slave owners will be able to sit down together at the table of brotherhood.

I have a dream that one day even the state of Mississippi, a state sweltering with the heat of injustice, sweltering with the heat of oppression, will be transformed into an oasis of freedom and justice.

I have a dream that my four little children will one day live in a nation where they will not be judged by the color of their skin but by the content of their character.

I have a dream today.

I have a dream that one day, down in Alabama, with its vicious racists, with its governor having his lips dripping with the words of interposition and nullification; one day right there in Alabama, little black boys and black girls will be able to join hands with little white boys and white girls as sisters and brothers.

I have a dream today.

Timeline

1957 – Martin receives the NAACP Spingarn Medal

1963 – Martin delivers his *I Have a Dream* speech

1964 – Martin is awarded the Nobel Peace Prize

1977 – Martin is posthumously presented the Presidential Medal of Freedom by President Jimmy Carter

1983 – President Ronald Reagan signed a bill creating a federal holiday to honor Martin

2004 – Martin was awarded the Congressional Gold Medal

minimovers.tv

 @marynhin   @GrowGrit
#minimoversandshakers

 Mary Nhin   Ninja Life Hacks

 Ninja Life Hacks

 @marynhin